First Printing
180Lyfe.com
180Lyfe LLC
1105 Shanarae Suite C
Killeen, TX
76549

A Word from our Founder
Archie J. Jenkins
180lyfe.com

This month has been remarkable with all the people I have met, as well as the interviews I've been doing. I have learned so much and it has definitely shown me that I am on the right path. With that, I am encouraged to continue to chase my dreams. I completely understand that quitting is not an option, but I sometimes wonder if I will be able to achieve what I am striving for. I know now without a shadow of a doubt that I can, and if I keep on, I will.

It has been an honor getting to know these amazing talents. Working with such high-profile clients and discussing their journey to stardom has been nothing short of inspirational. I can honestly say, when it comes to perfecting your gift, the people featured in this issue have mastered them. The most important lesson I learned is that consistency is the key. You want to be great? Be consistent, keep going no matter what adversities you may face. In today's times, adversities are to be expected, so you already know you have the ability to make it through.

I hope this issue inspires you as much as it did me. Remember to run your own race because you are your greatest competition. With that, you may have to be your biggest cheerleader as will, but YOU CAN DO IT, SO KEEP PUSHING

We want to hear from YOU! Please send us your questions and reviews to 180lyfe180show@gmail.com

Archie Jenkins a.k.a "Mr. 180" is a 33-year-old African American, Creative, and Entrepreneur. He is the owner of 180 Lyfe, and is a Photographer, Videographer, Motivational Speaker, Party Host, and the Executive Producer of the 180 SHow. The 180 SHow will introduce local entrepreneurs and will uncover how they started and the challenges they faced. He turned his life around after being convicted with felony charges for a crime he didn't commit.

Archie has always been a visionary with a heart to help others, but once he wrote the vision and made it plain, things began to shift in his life. He finally made a commitment to his purpose, passion, and dreams. Once he made the commitment to himself, giving back to others made an even greater impact. He believes that with persistence, faith in God, and prayer, all things are possible. Throughout all his adversity, Archie continues to help young people have their voice be heard by driving positive change in the community and around the world. His drive has led to speaking engagements for the youth and mentorship programs for all ages.

Archie is the Creator of 180 Lyfe Enterprise magazine. His goal is to be an inspiration to Entrepreneurs and Creatives of all generations. Archie J. Jenkins is known as Mr. 180, "the serial entrepreneur".

180LYFE.com

Proud Sponsors of
180Lyfe Enterprise Magazine

Angela Childress- Young
210- 451- 9553
www.spiritsheartchildcare.com

Lindy Jones
254-220-9543

Gloria Cooks - 979-219-7788

Dr. Cynthia Allen; 713-204-9554
Website: www.callenproductions.com
Email: callenproductions1@yahoo.com

www.cynthiajhickman.info

COME BE A PART OF OUR 1-YEAR PROMOTION PACKAGE

We are looking to keep great content your way we just need your help

737-212-2523 Or www.180lyfe.com
180Lyfe Enterprise Magazine

"I Believe in giving back 100% "

Ron Bivins

Real Estate Mogul – Ours Studios Owner - Movies, Documentaries, Filming, & Music

In 1970, Ron Bivins embarked on a new chapter of his life when he moved to Atlanta, GA. Four years later, in 1974, he delved into the world of real estate, guided by the wisdom of his mentor.

Through meticulous note-taking and unwavering determination, he immersed himself in the intricacies of the real estate game. Sitting down with Ron was a captivating experience, as he shared his vast knowledge and lived experiences, which spanned decades of history.

After achieving remarkable success in the real estate business, Ron ventured into the realm of film production, establishing his own production company that would later earn accolades for producing an award-winning documentary "As If We Were Ghosts" for Georgia Public Broadcasting for Juneteenth 2022 the aired in primetime, which highlighted Georgia sports from 1940-1970 that covered the period of segregated high school sports in Georgia. In our conversation, he passionately discussed the transformative changes he witnessed from the 1960s to the present day. Ron recounted his recent projects, while hinting at exciting new endeavors. As the Owner and CEO of Ours Studios, he proudly announced a collaboration with Richard Williams and his son Chavoita LaSane on Richard's documentary, not to tell the story of Venus and Serena, but to narrate his own captivating journey. Chavoita is a part of the Ours Studio team. Moreover, he expressed his delight in working with Monty Ross, the visionary behind 40 Acres and a Mule, who is actively engaged in multiple projects at the studio. For Ron, the power of a cohesive team is paramount, as it is the force that brings it all together. Undoubtedly, Ron Bivins personifies the essence of a true serial entrepreneur.

During our conversation, Ron delightfully shared an anecdote about his encounter with rapper Lil Yachty, acknowledging his limited familiarity with contemporary figures. Despite this, he commended Lil Yachty intellect, emphasizing the importance of staying connected with the current generation. Ron also regaled me with tales of the prestigious award shows he hosted and produced at Ours Studios, leaving me in awe of his creative prowess. Renowned for fostering community unity, Ours Studios has become the go-to destination in Atlanta.

As a passionate advocate for real estate development, Ron underscored how his success in this field enabled him to give back to the community. Expressing his deep concern for the food deficit issue, he emphasized his determination to eliminate the reliance on processed foods within the community. Ron believed that by rallying together, affluent individuals could ensure that all communities were adequately nourished, eradicating hunger among our most vulnerable, especially our children. It was in his eyes that I discerned the sincerity of his mission, and his words left a profound impact.

Ron also firmly believed that everyone needs a mentor. He spoke glowingly of Carter Coleman Sr., an esteemed educator who owned Atlanta oldest black real estate firm. Reflecting on his own journey, Ron vividly recounted how, at the age of 23, he achieved extraordinary financial success, which enabled him to open his own liquor store. However, a conversation with his wife compelled him to reconsider the impact of his actions on the community, propelling him to seek new avenues for his entrepreneurial pursuits. Adding to his list of accomplishments, Ron became Georgia's first black independent insurance agent. Encouraged by Mr. Coleman, he pursued this path, eventually joining the Georgia and Atlanta Independent Insurance Association. Although initially placed on the public relations committee to fulfill a token diversity requirement, Ron deftly transformed the opportunity into a steppingstone for his own success. Armed with dual licenses, he secured prominent clients such as Church's, Popeyes, McDonald's, C&S National Bank and many others solidifying his reputation in the commercial real estate industry in 1977 to present... Ron attributed his multifaceted achievements to his educational background in accounting, which bolstered his endeavors. Recounting the bustling activity at his studio, Ron confessed that he often encountered unfamiliar faces. To remain attuned to the evolving landscape, he emphasized the importance of providing opportunities to young talent, fostering a dynamic environment that embraced change. Ron's ability to adapt and mentor the next generation is a testament to his commitment to progress. His philosophy is simple but profound: to reach new heights, one must entrust the torch to others, enabling a relentless pursuit of the next level. Ron's face radiated joy when he spoke about how his aunt, Annie Bivins Jones stepped up to raise his sister, brother, and himself to allow his mother, Norris Bivins Curtis to get her college degree who rode the Trailways bus every morning for 4 ½ years, 37 miles to Albany State University at the age of 30. Families working together is significance and keeping God at the forefront of his life. Growing up in the projects in Americus, Georgia, he shared his trepidation when confronted with the opportunity to attend school alongside white peers. Although his potential acceptance to West Point was marred by the rampant segregation and racism of his hometown, these experiences underscored the importance of unity. Ron observed the systemic obstacles faced by the Black community in accessing loans, thus highlighting the urgency of uplifting, and supporting our own. He vehemently believed that life should not be measured solely by wealth or material possessions, challenging the societal paradigm that equates success with affluence. His piercing words resonated deeply with me, reminding me of the significance of collective progress. Moreover, Ron expressed his heartfelt desire to redefine the narrative and dispel the stereotypes that have plagued the Black community for far too long. He lamented the prevalence of profit-driven endeavors that perpetuate disrespect within our own ranks, urging a shift toward positive actions. Ron firmly believed that our strength as a race lies in giving back, and he remains steadfast in his commitment to leading by example. Ron's passion for transforming communities and eradicating the negative stigmas associated with his race was truly awe-inspiring.

In closing, Ron shared his experiences in starting a business, the importance of building business credit, and the necessity of seizing opportunities. He candidly remarked that one must actively pursue one's goals, as success is not bestowed upon anyone. His words resonated as a guiding principle for life. Ron Bivins is a trailblazer whose remarkable journey transcends the boundaries of time. With his unwavering determination, commitment to community, and relentless pursuit of positive change, he has built a legacy that exemplifies the transformative power of entrepreneurship. Ours Studios stands as a testament to his vision, a haven where individuals converge, dreams are nurtured, and the collective strength of the community is harnessed. Ron Bivins, an extraordinary individual inspiring other to believe in their potential and embrace the limitless possibilities that lie ahead.

www.oursstudios.com

PRESENTED BY MISS M

DATE
NOV
11
2023

TIME
12NOON
TO 7PM

2ND ANNUAL BOSSITUP
EXTRAVAGANZA
VENDOR/FASHION
SHOW

PLACE: INFUSION DANCE & EVENT CENTER
15635 VISION DR. STE 100 PFLUGERVILLE, TX 78660
HOST: MISS MARGARET NEALY
HOSTED BY: ARCHIE J. JENKINS, DJ QUAN

SCAN FOR
TICKETS

PERFORMANCE:
BEAUX BABY, BRIAN SEAGRAVES, MS. D1V1NITY

TICKETS ARE ON SALE ON EVENTBRITE FOR $10

Delsina A West CWP, M.S., CPT, P.N.
Certified Wellness Practitioner
Nutrition and Fitness Coach

For more tips or if you have questions go to www.dwestcoaching.com and be sure to check out my podcast "Fine, Fit and Fabulous" anywhere you get your podcasts.

Men's Health

Let us take a moment this month to focus on Men's health. Men's health issues can be quite complex and varied, and it is essential to understand them to take appropriate steps towards improving overall health and well-being. In this article, I will discuss the top 5 men's health issues that affect millions of men worldwide.

1. Heart disease: Heart disease is one of the most significant health concerns for men. It is a condition that affects the heart and its function, leading to a range of complications, such as heart attacks and stroke. Men are at a higher risk of developing heart disease due to factors such as high blood pressure, high cholesterol, obesity, and smoking.
2. Prostate Cancer: Prostate cancer is a common cancer that affects men worldwide. It is a slow-growing cancer that develops in the prostate gland, which is a small gland that produces seminal fluid. Symptoms may include frequent urination, difficulty starting or stopping urination, and blood in the urine. Men over the age of 50 are at higher risk of developing prostate cancer.
3. Mental Health: Mental health issues can be significant concerns for men. Men are less likely to seek help for mental health issues, which can lead to more severe problems, including depression, anxiety, and substance abuse. It is essential to seek help if you feel you are struggling with mental health issues.
4. Diabetes: Diabetes is a condition that affects the way the body processes sugar. It can lead to complications such as nerve damage, blindness, and heart disease. Men are at a higher risk of developing diabetes due to factors such as obesity, poor diet, and lack of exercise.
5. Erectile Dysfunction: Erectile dysfunction is a condition where a man is unable to achieve or maintain an erection for sexual activity. It can be caused by factors such as low testosterone, high blood pressure, and diabetes. It can have a significant impact on a man's quality of life and relationships.

It is important that men pay close attention to their health especially as they get older. By understanding the top 5 issues, you can take appropriate steps towards prevention and treatment. Maintaining a healthy lifestyle, seeking medical help when needed, and regular check-ups can go a long way in ensuring good health and well-being.

Sponsorship Package Exclusive:

$350

*Logo on entrance backdrop
*One (1) full page advertisement in upcoming 180Lyfe Enterprise Magazine
*Sponsorship shoutout on the 180SHow
*One (1) ticket to the Night of Elegance Awards Gala
Email: 180lyfe180show@gmail.com

R&B SINGER, MUSICIAN, SONGWRITER, PRODUCER AND ACTOR

GARY "G7" JENKINS

KNOWN AS LIL G" FROM THE R&B GROUP SILK

R&B superstar and SILK frontman Gary "'Lil G" Jenkins.
Born and raised in Nashville, Tennessee, this musical genius started
singing in church at the early age of seven, which earned him a role as a
featured soloist on The Bobby Jones Gospel Show for many years to
follow. At the age of nine and only a few lessons, Gary E. Jenkins
mastered the guitar, which engraved a new appreciation for the art. That
was truly the unleashing, as his gift expanded into fourteen instruments,
including an assortment of keyboards, drums, guitars, etc. (most of
which have been self taught).

While attending Tennessee State University (TSU) in Nashville, Gary
majored in music, with an emphasis in piano and voice. As a member of
the prestigious TSU Jazz Ensemble, he was selected to accompany Dizzy
Gillespie on piano, during his visit to the school. In addition, he appeared
in several opera productions and performed with the popular TSU
marching band.

In transitioning this love for music into a career, Gary formed a band and
began performing in and around the Nashville area, winning the National
Budweiser Showdown.

In 1992, Gary answered an audition call and earned the lead singer role
for the newly signed R&B group, Silk. Their career began with the success
of the decade's most memorable single, the legendary "Freak Me", which
was a chart topper across the board for months. The song was one of
their many releases from their 1993 debut album Lose Control. With new
musical presence,

Gary established himself as a multi-talented songwriter, producer and
instrumentalist, resulting in phenomenal success for the group. Their career
spanned the globe for nearly ten years, with more than five million records
sold. The success of their sophomore album, Silk, led to the follow-up,

Tonight. Remaining consistent, they released their fourth album, Love
Sessions. Gary gained national recognition with his appearances on Jay Leno,
Regis and Kathi Lee, MTV, BET, Soul Train, Jenny Jones, Ricky Lake, Moesha,
Showtime At The Apollo, Motown Live and, to name a few. Achieving
international acclaim, Gary has toured throughout the world in such
countries as Japan, Korea, the United Kingdom, Canada, Mexico, France, the
Netherlands and Germany.

Returning to his roots, Gary resigned from the group in 2002 to persue his
first love: the passion of true musicianship. Over an eighteen month period,
he wrote, recorded and produced, with live instruments, his first
independent, solo project: The Other Side.

Currently touring in various venues throughout the US, Gary is establishing
himself in a class with a few of today's hottest artists who share the title of
pure musicianship — Alicia Keys, India Arie and Lenny Kravitz, to name a few.

He has since appeared in numerous musicals, such as Fake Friends, Perilous
Times, Secret Lovers, and the popular Tyler Perry's Ma Dear's Family Reunion,
which were on national tours, periodically, from 1997 through 2002. After
experiencing solo success Gary returned to SILK and they are currently
working on new music. Currently, Gary is working on his upcoming solo
project G7 "No Parole" and has released his first single "That's My Baby" on
September 7, 2021. There's no stopping this lyrical genius so sit back and get
ready!

NEW RELEASE
"That's My Baby"

AVAILABLE
EVERYWHERE!

FACEBOOK
@GARYLILGJENKINS

INSTAGRAM
@GARYLILG

TWITTER
@GARYGJENKINS

Morgan Family Practice
&
Home Care Services, PLLC

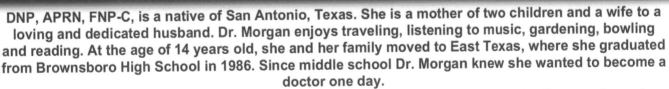

Dr. Chrisettia Morgan

San Antonio, Tx - Worldwide

DNP, APRN, FNP-C, is a native of San Antonio, Texas. She is a mother of two children and a wife to a loving and dedicated husband. Dr. Morgan enjoys traveling, listening to music, gardening, bowling and reading. At the age of 14 years old, she and her family moved to East Texas, where she graduated from Brownsboro High School in 1986. Since middle school Dr. Morgan knew she wanted to become a doctor one day.

After graduating from high school, she enrolled into Tyler Junior College in Tyler Texas, where she begins to pursue her dream. Dr. Morgan decided to enroll into perquisites for the RN nursing program because there was a waiting list for the LVN program. Dr. Morgan knew at this point that she needed to graduate with sone type of degree, so the following semester she graduated with her Early Childhood Education Associate Degree which was far from why she initially attended college. She worked as an elementary special education teachers aid for a few years while continuing to pursue her nursing degree.

She decided to move to Fort Worth, Texas to live with her aunt and while there, received her Medical Assistant Certificate. At this point she was married with 2 children and continued to pursue her dream to become a doctor.

In 2002, Dr. Morgan attained her LVN certificate from Concorde Colleges. She continued to take perquisites for her RN degree at Tarrant County College (TCC) in Fort Worth, Texas. She applied for the RN program and was denied entrance related to that her sciences were greater than 5 years old and she would need to repeat those sciences before reapplying. Dr. Morgan began her search for collages which did not require a time frame for science classes.

In 2006, she attained her Registered Nurse Associate degree from Vernon College in Wichita Falls and continued to pursue her dream.

In 2010, she graduated from Texas Tech University with her Bachelor of Science in Nursing. She worked at Baylor Scott & White All Saints Hospital in Fort Worth, Texas as a charge nurse and house supervisor for 7 years while continuing to pursue her Master of Science in Nursing and Post Masters in Family Nurse Practitioner degree. Dr. Morgan graduated from Walden University with her master's degree in nursing 2016.

In 2019, she returned back to San Antonio.

In 2020, she completed her Doctor in Nursing Practice degree from Walden University and began her own mobile health business (Morgan Family Practice & Home Care Services, PLLC). We offer practitioner home visits, concierge services, lab services and IV hydration and wellness services. This journey was not easy. However, because of my dedication and perseverance, I completed this journey with a 4.0 GPA. I'm grateful to God for every opportunity and obstacle because I wouldn't be where I am today without him by my side.

Facebook: Chrisettia Morgan

Vibin with Ang

Host: Coach Ang

Mathew 9:37

My passion is bringing people together.
I will be helping black women rekindle their relationship with black men.
This will be a production encouraging and uplifting our community of people.

Angela Young-
Business Coach
Entrepreneur

Coming Summer
2023

Fb: Vibin WithAng

Vibinwithang@gmail.com

Jorel "JFly" Flynn:
A Musical Force Transforming Lives

Jorel "JFly" Flynn is a remarkable individual who is making a profound impact on people's lives through his unwavering passion for music. As a CEO, philanthropist, humanitarian, community activist, husband, and father, he embodies the spirit of an artist dedicated to uplifting others.

Originally hailing from Waycross, Georgia, JFly began his musical journey as a talented drummer and band leader. Soon after graduating from high school, he made his way to Atlanta, where he wasted no time in leaving a lasting impression on the city's vibrant music scene.

Throughout his career, JFly has established himself as a versatile studio musician, lending his exceptional skills to various musical genres. Working alongside the likes of After7, Andre 3000, Montel Jordan, and the legendary Aretha Franklin, he has contributed to numerous iconic recordings.

In addition to his role as a studio musician, JFly's talent as a musical director has brought major festivals to his hometown in Waycross, Georgia. His directorial achievements extend beyond live performances, encompassing television appearances on esteemed shows such as the Top Rated WSB Centennial Olympic Park's 4th of July Celebration, the Heisman Trophy Awards, Soul Train Music Awards, BET's Sunday's Best, and Tyler Perry Movies.

Bobby Brown & JFly   Montel Jordan   Patti LaBelle   Peabo Bryson

"The catalyst for embarking on my current journey was the realization of my limited knowledge about the music industry and the strong desire I harbored to pursue a professional career as a musician."
-JFLy

Ig & FB: 1jfly

Sit down with JFLY

Beyond his musical achievements, JFly has also made significant contributions as a businessman and advocate for the music community. Notably, he served as the President of the Recording Academy® Atlanta Chapter and co-chair of the Education committee. His involvement in the implementation of the Music Modernization Act, which modernized laws for the music industry, underscores his commitment to improving the landscape for fellow musicians. Collaborating with celebrity artists, musicians, and esteemed Recording Academy members, JFly has engaged with commissioners and national leaders on Capitol Hill to champion the rights and interests of the music community.

However, JFly's dedication does not end there. His philanthropic efforts have led him to invest his time and talent in the youth of his community.
In 2009, he embarked on his most passionate endeavor, the "How Big Is Your Dream!?" Foundation.
Through this initiative, he empowers local youth to transform their dreams into reality by providing educational resources, practical application opportunities, and fostering engagement.

Jorel "JFly" Flynn is a true force to be reckoned with, using his multifaceted talents to shape lives and leave an indelible mark on the world. His unwavering commitment to music, philanthropy, and advocacy makes him a beacon of inspiration for aspiring artists and a pillar of hope for communities in need. As a CEO, philanthropist, humanitarian, community activist, husband, and father, JFly continues to make a difference, one beat at a time. A pivotal moment for JFly occurred when he witnessed former student artists returning as counselors after graduating. Their desire to give back and help upcoming students confirmed that he was making a positive impact and instilling important values in the kids he worked with. Seeing this "pay it forward" mentality filled him with pride and gratitude. He emphasized that it was crucial for him not to name the foundation after himself but rather to establish its own unique identity— "How Big Is Your Dream?!" He discussed both the growth of the nonprofit organization and his personal brand.

JFly Music Group, LLC
180Lyfe Enterprise July 2023

What does culture mean to you and what part of culture do you play?

To me, culture encompasses the knowledge and traditions that are passed down through generations, shaping and influencing our communities. I am passionate about sharing my expertise and industry knowledge in the music industry with aspiring individuals who want to pursue careers in this field. My focus is on providing access, training, and guidance from professionals to empower the next generation.

So, tell us about some stages you have been on?!

Speaking of stages, I've been on, I have had the opportunity to work on various movies such as "I Can Do Bad All By Myself," "A Family That Preys," and "Aretha Franklins Genius." Additionally, I served as the music director for the live band at the Heisman Trophy Awards and performed at events like the Soul Train Awards, Sunday Best, and the Atlanta Centennial Park 4th of July Fireworks Celebration. I also organized my own festival in my hometown of Waycross, GA for eight consecutive years. Furthermore, I had the privilege of being involved in the 2018 Music Modernization Act, which aimed to update copyright laws and create a fairer system.

What's next for you?

As for what's next, my focus is on continuing to create opportunities for the next generation of aspiring individuals seeking careers in the music industry.

Bobby Brown, Tony Terry, Howard Hewett – Notable Jazz musicians

Jennifer Holliday

Johnny Gill

Music Modernization Act

Deborah Cox
Kevon Edmonds

Malcolm Jamal Warner

FB & IG
HBIYD
JFly The Flytrap,
How Big Is Your Dream Foundation

JFly, leads a highly active and engaging lifestyle with a multitude of programs and activities focused on music, arts, diversity, and education. Alongside their summer program, they also manage a one-week spring break academy called M.A.D.E. (Music Arts Diversity and Education). Furthermore, during the winter season, JFly organizes a noteworthy event called U.N.I.TY (You & I Tie) for Teens by Teens, which originated from the successful ladies' night out and fellas' night out events.

JFly is not only a talented individual, but he is also a loving husband and a devoted father. The moment he mentions his family, a warm smile lights up his face, revealing the deep significance they hold in his life. Despite the challenges of finding time for a vacation, he emphasizes that his children understand his commitment as a parent and the importance of his work. Juggling responsibilities and achieving balance is a skill he has learned and values greatly. Undoubtedly, family takes precedence for him.

Reflecting on his children's growth, JFly marvels at how quickly they have bloomed before his very eyes. His wife and children have been incredibly supportive, which adds an extra layer of joy to his journey. While discussing his offspring, he proudly reveals that he is happily married and blessed with four remarkable children—three daughters aged 14, 8, and 6, and a 2-year-old son. JFly mentions their shared passion for sports, particularly track and volleyball, and hints that they are also talented in music. His beaming smile conveys volumes about the pride and love he feels for his family.

"Becoming an entrepreneur was not something I actively pursued, but as I started to achieve financial success in the industry, I realized the importance of establishing a sustainable career. This led me to form an LLC, JFly Music Group, to protect my personal assets and formalize my business operations."
-JFLY

JFly emphasizes the importance of intentional scheduling in his life. Although he acknowledges the need to decline certain opportunities, he remains dedicated to his family's well-being. He firmly expresses his belief in not forcing his children into any specific career path but ensuring they have a clear direction if they choose to enter the industry. He mentions that they also participate in the summer academy, further nurturing their interests and talents.

Despite facing financial difficulties and contemplating giving up, JFly refused to accept failure as an option. He drew motivation from those who doubted his aspirations and used it as fuel to prove them wrong. He invested personal funds to push forward and make his dream a reality. Reflecting on the hurdles and early stages he overcame to secure federal trademark recognition, JFly becomes emotional, his eyes welling up with tears. Yet, he remains steadfast in his determination, acknowledging that he saw the dream and recognized his destiny, refusing to let anyone hinder his progress. He encourages others to seize their own dreams and pursue them with unwavering determination.

JFly's inspiring journey exemplifies the power of family, perseverance, and the belief in making dreams come true.

www.howbigisyourdream.org

Tierra Pitchford

My name is Tierra Pitchford, I am a wife to D'Jon Pitchford. A mother to three beautiful children, DJ, Amari and Dylan. I am also an educator in the Pflugerville School District, teaching 1st grade. I am a graduate student at Texas State University, a part of the Scholastic Black Advisory Board as well as the 2022-2023 Scholastic Teacher Fellows program. What inspires me is, my students daily with the things they achieve and continuous effort they put towards their work. In 2023, I will continue my Master's Degree in Education with a principal certification. Build on my leadership skills and accomplish goals I set out for myself. As Nelson Mandela stated, Education is the most powerful weapon which you can use to change the world, that's why education is important to me. An influential woman to me means someone that is going to uplift, guide and motivate others no matter the circumstances. My daily service and commitment as an educator are what I bring to the community. I was also a part of the Executive Board for the Central Texas Wolves Youth Sports Organization.

Ig: @determinedtee
FB: Tierra Pitchford

**Educator
1st Grade Team
Lead Teacher**

To our future generations, continue to set and accomplish goals. Do not fear failure, set out to achieve the unthinkable, and even if it doesn't work out how you want it to the 1st time continue to push. Establish a habit of self-reflection in order to be able to critically think about the positives and negatives of yourself that could be changed or not.

"I measure success by the people you love in your life and the true, loving friends you have, as well as the number of other people you have helped along the way."

Shirley Jones of The Jones Girls

Detroit – Atlanta * Grammy nominated singer *

In 1979 The Jones Girls "You Gonna Make Me Love Somebody Else" showed Gamble and Huff still had the magic touch. The classic went top ten on Billboards' R&B and Disco Charts. However, lead singer Shirley Jones and sisters Brenda and Valorie were not new to the game. Gospel singer Mary Frazier Jones groomed her daughter's unique harmonies when they were babies in their hometown Detroit.

By the time Shirley and her sisters signed with Philadelphia International Records, they were teenage veterans. The Jones Girls traveled the world for several years with fellow Detroiter Diana Ross as her backup singers. Ms. Ross even let the girls shine with their own spot where they sang "If I Ever Lose This Heaven". Diana Ross told Gamble and Huff that The Jones Girls were too good to be anybody's back-up singers forever.

Those Philly years provided Shirley and her sisters with a string of hits. They include "Who Can I Run To", "I Just Love The Man", "Dance Turned Into A Romance" and their Grammy-Nominated classic "Nights Over Egypt". After a brief unsuccessful stay at RCA Records, The Jones Girls decided to take a hiatus. Brenda got married and Valorie entered college. But Shirley still wanted to sing.

She returned to Philadelphia International Records in 1985 as a solo artist. Shirleys' 1986 Debut album "Always In The Mood" proved she could handle the spotlight alone. Her 1986 classic "Do You Get Enough Love" stayed number one on Billboards R&B Chart for Three weeks!!!

"Proven to be prophetic, 'Do You Get Enough Love' Shirley married and embarked on a new career while raising her son Cameron, who now stands at an impressive height of over 6'7". Shirley made a triumphant return to the stage in 2011, touring with The O'Jays. In October 2015, she released her new album, 'My Time to Shine,' featuring a duet with the late, great Mel Waiters and a remake of the Jones Girls' classic, 'I'm At Your Mercy.' The following year, Shirley took on the role of Mrs. Henderson in Shelly Garrett's 30-year anniversary production of the iconic play 'Beauty Shop.' On July 1st, 2017, she performed at the Essence Festival alongside Mary J. Blige, Chaka Khan, Lalah Hathaway, and other artists for 'Mary's Strength of a Woman Night.' Shirley made a memorable appearance on Tom Joyner's Fantastic Voyage Cruise in 2018. In October 2019, she delighted audiences with three sold-out shows in London, performing at the renowned Indigo 02 arena, the historic Jazz Café, and the iconic Fairfield Hall in Croydon. In 2020, the story of The Jones Girls will be featured on TV One's popular show 'Unsung' as part of the fall episodes. Stay tuned! Shirley is sure to entertain you in true old-school style, showcasing her sass, class, and superb musicianship. Take a nostalgic journey with Shirley as she performs the songs that she and her sisters made famous, capturing a time of love and pure fun."

Facebook & Instagram
@shirleyjonesofthejonesgirls

A Word from
Shirley Jones

"I am thrilled to announce that I have a new album coming out titled 'In Loving Memory.' It serves as a tribute to my sisters Brenda and Valorie, also known as The Jones Girls. I have been working on this album during the pandemic, and I cannot wait for the world to hear it. My hope is that everyone enjoys it as much as I did recording it. I wanted to ensure that their legacy lives on. Additionally, I have some exciting performances lined up, including Soul Train Cruise 2024, Portugal 2024, United Kingdom 2024, and Greece 2024."

"My passion for singing was ignited as a child when I sang Gospel music with my mom and sisters. Last year, I was honored by the National R&B Society. My first album achieved Platinum certification, and the hit single 'Nights Over Egypt' was certified Gold."

"I hold a special place in my heart for those advocating for gun control, supporting individuals dealing with mental challenges, and educators enlightening our youth. Their dedication and efforts inspire me. I firmly believe that children are our future, and it is essential to teach them well and empower them to lead the way."

"To God be the glory for all that He has done.
I wouldn't have this career if it weren't for Him!"

In my business endeavors, I adhere to three fundamental principles

Always negotiate in good faith

Honor your word and stick to your commitments,

Treat everyone the way you want to be treated when engaging in negotiations."

Facebook & Instagram
@shirleyjonesofthejonesgirls

FROM: DR. CYNTHIA J. HICKMAN- YOUR PROACTIVE CAREGIVER ADVOCATE

WEBSITE: HTTPS://CYNTHIAJHICKMAN.INFO

AUTHOR, SPEAKER, NURSE EDUCATOR, CAREGIVER ADVOCATE, BLOGGER, PODCASTER

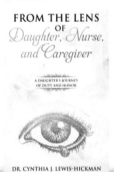

Available on Amazon

Speaking Topics:

Nursing Education

Nutritional Health in the Elderly

Chronic Disease Management

Academic Writing/Editing (APA)

Caregiving Tips & Strategies

Continuum Of Caregiving

Social Media:

LinkedIn

Facebook

Medium

Instagram

Spotify

713-569-5294

Brilliant Moments

&

Handz of Faith

Collaboration

Now offering Travel

Spa Packages

Ask us about the packages we offer

Tierra Pitchford

Brilliant Moments

512-785-4856

Stephanie Martin

Handz of Faith

512-677-8633

Travel Spa Party
Packages

Package 1

20 minute massage (3 ladies)

Balloon Setup

Table Linens

Table Decor

Package 2

30 minute massage (6 ladies)

Balloon Setup

Table Linens

Table Decor

Ask about our other packages and add-ons we offer!

Contact
Tierra Pitchford
Brilliant Moments
512-785-4856
Or
Stephanie Martin
Handz of Faith
512-677-8633

Tyron Perry
T.I.E. Massage LLC

6601 Cypresswood Dr Ste 102 Spring, TX 77379
M-F 9 am - 7 pm
Sat 9-1

"My Mission is to provide professional massage therapy. I have 18yrs of experience. I'm here to help you relax, unwind and rejuvenate. I want to help you recover faster and help reduce pain with customized massage."

281-466-7768

Ask me about my specials! Book Now!!

Made in the USA
Columbia, SC
24 July 2024

38627783R00018